Saint Joan the Girl in Armour

Written by Dorothy Smith

Illustrated by Robert Broomfield

PAULIST PRESS
New York/New Jersey

For LEILA
with love

First published in Great Britain in 1988 by McCrimmon Publishing Co Ltd, Great Wakering Essex England. Published in 1990 in the United States of America by Paulist Press, 997 Macarthur Boulevard, Mahwah, New Jersey 07430.

© 1988 Dorothy Smith

All rights reserved. No part of this book may be reproduced or transmitted in any form or by any means, electronic or mechanical, including photocopying, recording or by any information storage and retrieval system without permission in writing from the Publisher.

Library of Congress Cataloging-in-Publication Data

Smith, Dorothy.
    Saint Joan: the girl in armour/by Dorothy Smith.
      p. cm.
    Illustrated by Robert Broomfield.
    Summary: A biography of the young French woman who, inspired by visions supposedly from God, led the French army against English invaders, was burned at the stake as a heretic, and eventually was declared a saint.
    ISBN 0-8091-6594-5
    1. Joan, of Arc, Saint, 1412-1431—Juvenile literature.
2. Christian saints—France—Biography—Juvenile literature.
3. France—History—Charles VII, 1422-1461—Juvenile literature. [1. Joan, of Arc, Saint, 1412-1431. 2. Saints.]
    I. Broomfield, Robert, 1930-   ill. II. Title.
DC103.5.S55   1990
944'.026'092—dc20   89-49289
    [B]   CIP
                                                                              AC

Cover design Robert Broomfield

Printed in Hong Kong.

Contents

1. 'We have burnt a saint!'   5
2. The village girl   7
3. The voices   12
4. France and England   16
5. The mission   21
6. The Dauphin at Chinon   28
7. The Maid of Orleans   33
8. The coronation   39
9. On to Paris   43
10. Capture   47
11. The prisoner on trial   49
12. The end   57
13. Joan of France   59

1. 'We have burnt a saint!'

ON A DAY at the end of May, all the houses in the French town of Rouen were empty as the townspeople—ten thousand of them—crowded into the market place. They stood silent, for they were held back by a thousand of the English soldiers who occupied France, so they dared not shout or make any demonstration.

The church bells were tolling when between the lines of soldiers appeared a young girl, exhausted and pale, in a long gown, with a hood over her short black hair. Two priests walked with her. She knew, and all the onlookers knew, that she was being led to her death.

She looked round at the waiting crowds, and at the town of Rouen, where she had spent five desperately unhappy months. 'Oh, Rouen,' she sighed, 'I am afraid you will suffer because of my death!'

In the market place stood a tall stake surrounded by a vast pile of wood, and over it hung a placard declaring that it was prepared for 'Joan, who called herself the Maid, who is a liar, a deceiver of the people, a blasphemer of God, a witch---'

The girl Joan knelt and prayed beside it, praying

for herself and her enemies, and for the people of France. Especially she called Saint Michael, Saint Catherine and Saint Margaret to protect her.

The Bishop of Beauvais rose to his feet. He declared that this girl was cast out by the Church and abandoned. She was to be handed over to the military authorities. The English, who were in charge of the execution, got impatient at the formalities. They only wanted to see her dead. 'Are we to be kept here till dinner time?' they shouted.

Joan was bundled to the stake and tied to it. She asked if she might have a cross, and an English soldier broke a stick of wood in half, tied the pieces together and gave it to her. She kissed it and put it in the folds of her gown. One of the priests who was with her hurried into the nearby church and came out with the cross they carried in processions. He climbed beside her and held it before her eyes.

'Away with her!' called the town governor, and the executioner set light to the wood.

Joan was alarmed, and called to the priest who held the cross: 'Get down! You will be burnt!' He clambered down, but held the cross high where she could see it as long as she could see anything.

Soon the crowd could not see her for the smoke and the flames, but they heard her call out 'Jesus! Jesus!' It was the last word she spoke.

Later the executioner went back to the stake, took her ashes and all that remained and threw everything into the River Seine.

That night a cloud of doubt and remorse hung like a cloud of smoke over the city of Rouen. Why had this young girl been sent to her death by the Church she loved? Why had her fellow countrymen not tried to save her from the English when she had fought so bravely against them herself? Even the English wondered if great countries won battles by burning nineteen-year-old girls.

An English soldier spoke for them all. 'We are lost,' he said. 'We have burnt a saint!'

2. The village girl

THE FEAST of the Three Kings—the Epiphany—the Twelfth Day of Christmas, January 6th, was always celebrated cheerfully and noisily in the little village of Domremy in eastern France. In one particular year, 1412, as the villagers ran about calling greetings to one another so loudly that the cocks woke up and started crowing, a little girl was born. Long afterwards the people said they were rejoicing at her birth; but of course they did not know then that the baby would ever be famous. She was just the daughter of their neighbour, Jacques d'Arc.

Jacques and his wife Isabelle had come to Domremy from a village a few miles away, and had settled there. He was a farmer, like most of the villagers, and he owned some cows and sheep, some farm horses and a good many pigs. Sometimes Jacques acted as spokesman for the village, on official business, and he went to the nearby town of Vaucouleurs, to see the governor, Robert de Baudricourt. So Jacques was a respected man in the community, and not badly off. There was always enough for the family to eat; but Domremy was a poor village, and life was never easy. The family lived in a small stone house with a smoky open fire, no windows, and no lamps in winter, only smelly candles. The only life lying ahead for his daughter seemed to be poverty and hard work, settled down as the wife of a local man.

The village church was very close to their house. It was named after St Remy, who was also the patron of the great cathedral of Reims, where French Kings were crowned. The new baby was baptised in the little church; she had a great many godmothers and godfathers, ten altogether, which shows that her family were liked and respected in the village.

She was named Jeanne, and she was known as Jeanne d'Arc, after her father. Years later, when she was known in England as well as in France, the English called her Joan—JOAN OF ARC.

Joan did not go to school, and never learned to read, but she was brought up to work hard, like all the village children. 'My parents brought me up very strictly,' she said later. Her mother taught her at home, and she learned to clean the house and to scrub. As she grew older she learned to sew and to spin, and she was quite proud of her skill. 'I feared no woman as a rival, with the needle or the spindle,' she said.

And when her mother had nothing for her to do, or at busy times, she was sent out to help her father. She dug the vegetables and helped at haymaking and harvest, and she took the cows and sheep out to pasture, or the pigs to feed in the beech woods. Like the other children, she had to take her turn staying with the beasts to look after them, in case they were attacked by marauding bands of robbers or wandering soldiers.

Because she had to look after the animals, sometimes people have thought of Joan as a pretty little shepherdess, rather like Bo Peep. But life was certainly not like that in the hard working village of Domremy, and Joan was no pretty doll in a sun bonnet. She was not very tall, but a firm, stocky little girl, with black hair and a sunburnt face, wearing a red dress like all the other girls.

Joan had two brothers, older than she was, called Jacquemin, and Jean, and one younger brother, called Pierre. Her only sister had died, but her great friend was a little girl called Hauviette, and they were very fond of each other.

In spite of the hard work, the children had some fun. There was an old ruined castle by the river, where they sometimes drove the animals, to be safe; and there they would play at battles between the French and the English.

There was a special tree in the forest, called Le Beau May, where people said you could see the little people, the fairies, who knew about magic. There was a spring beside it, like a wishing well. The children used to go there and hang garlands on the branches, and dance and sing. When she was a little girl, Joan used to go along with them. But as she grew older, she thought it was rather silly and she gave it up.

Though she never learnt to read, her mother taught her to say the Our Father and the Hail Mary and the Creed, and she went to church on Sundays

and Holy Days. She seems to have been a good little girl, and she was well liked in the village, although the other children teased her and said she was too serious and pious.

Years later, the villagers remembered her kindly: 'She was modest, simple, devout, and went gladly to church and to sacred places; she worked, sewed, hoed in the fields, and did what was needful about the house,' they recalled.

One sacred place she liked to go to was in the forest, about two miles from home. The forest was dangerous. Wolves and wild boar sometimes appeared, and there might be robbers, who were even more of a threat; so Joan's mother did not approve of her daughter slipping away. But sometimes she was able to. Then she went to a little shrine, a tiny chapel hidden among the trees, called Notre Dame de Bermont. There was a crucifix and a statue of Our Lady with Baby Jesus. Joan liked to sit still and look at them, and enjoyed a quiet time on her own.

3. The voices

ONE DAY, when she was twelve years old, Joan's life changed forever as something happened to make her different from all other girls. She had been watching the sheep with some of her friends, and they had been running races. Joan was out of breath and sat down to rest, when a boy told her her mother wanted her. Joan hurried home; but her mother was cross because she had left the sheep.

'Didn't you send for me?' Joan asked. Her mother said she had not. Joan supposed the boy was teasing her, and began to make her way back. She was crossing her father's garden when it happened. This is how she described it, seven years later when she was being questioned about this amazing experience:

'I was in my thirteenth year when God sent a Voice to guide me. At first I was very much frightened. The Voice came towards the hour of noon, in summer, in my father's garden. I heard the Voice on my right hand, in the direction of the church. I seldom hear it without seeing a light. That light always appears on the side from which I hear the Voice.'

At first she only heard a voice, speaking to her from a burst of blazing light, and she was frightened. But soon she began to see figures, the Beings to whom the Voices belonged, and she was comforted by this. She recognised them, and they spoke to each other by name, she said.

The first figure was St Michael, the Archangel, who led the angels against the Devil when he tried to invade Heaven, and thrust him out. St Michael is described in the Bible as the leader of heavenly armies against the forces of evil. He told her she must be a good girl and go to church, and God would help her. Perhaps she wondered why a shining angel was needed to tell her that; but he went on to say that God had a special task for her. Two more figures were going to appear to her, and she must obey them exactly, for they had a message for her from Our Lord Himself.

The two saints came, and they were St Catherine and St Margaret. A thousand years before, St Catherine had died rather than give up her Christian faith. At her trial she had explained her belief to her non-Christian judges. 'Their heads were crowned with fair crowns, richly and preciously,' Joan said. Now her Voices, and the saints, came to her every day, sometimes more than once a day. Joan lost her fear of them and was happy when they appeared, and wept when they left her. She was allowed to embrace them, and kneeling before them she embraced their knees. Whenever they appeared, she smelt a soft and fragrant perfume.

Often they came to her when the church bells were ringing. Joan had always loved the sound of church bells, and paused to listen to them when she was in the house or out in the fields.

Joan gave these accounts of her Voices years later, but at the time she said nothing—not to her parents, nor to the parish priest at the church of St Remy, nor to Hauviette or any of the other children; yet these Voices spoke to her every day for five years. Very soon they told her the special task she had been chosen to perform.

Their message was extraordinary. She was to get a horse and armour and go to the aid of the uncrowned King of France! She was to make sure he was crowned, and she was to drive the invading English out of the fair land of France.

She, Joan the village girl who had never been more than a few miles away from home! At first she could not believe it, and protested that she was only a poor country girl who knew nothing of war. But gently and firmly the Voices insisted it must be so. It would not happen until she was a little older, but God would decide when the time was ready, and the Voices would tell her what to do, so that she could save France.

Save France! How could France need her help?

4. France and England

WHEN she was a little girl, Joan would hear her father and the other men talking about France, but she had never paid much attention. She just knew that England and France were at war, and that English troops wandered over the countryside, robbing and looting. That was why it was so important to have guards looking after the animals in the fields. She knew the boys from Domremy had battles with the boys from the next village, calling themselves French and English.

Now she listened closely, to find out what was wrong with France and what God expected her to do about it.

When a new King came to the throne of France, he was crowned in the great Cathedral at Reims. There he was anointed with holy oil, said to have been blessed by St Remy himself. Until that day he was not truly King. In Joan's time, the old King of France had died, and been succeeded by his son. That son had never been to Reims, so to many Frenchmen he was not yet King—he was only Charles the Dauphin, which was the title given to the King's eldest son.

Though France was a kingdom, it was divided into huge estates, owned and ruled over by mighty dukes and other noblemen. They acknowledged the King, but they all behaved as if they were kings themselves; so the real King was weak and powerless, and France was in a terrible state of confusion.

While France was weak, the kings of England claimed that they should be kings of France too, and take over the kingdom. For nearly a hundred years they had forced their demands, invaded France with their armies, and won many battles.

In 1415, three years after Joan was born, the warlike English King, Henry V, had defeated the French at the battle of Agincourt. The French had been forced to sign a peace treaty, giving up their land to King Henry, who married the French Princess Katharine and called himself King of France.

The plans of kings do not always work out. In 1422, the year when Joan was ten years old, Henry V died, and his son, a baby only a few months old, became King Henry VI of England and France—though of course the English generals and nobles really held power. They and their troops occupied land all over France.

In the very same year, the King of France, Charles VI, who everyone said was old and mad, died too. His son, who was nineteen years old, claimed to be King—Charles VII; but he was a weak, uncertain young man, who could not even manage to get to Reims for his coronation, the one thing that would have made the French people really believe he was King. Paris, his capital city, was in the hands of the English, so he could not rule from there, but moved around from one castle to another.

The chief nobles of France saw this muddle as a splendid chance to become more powerful themselves. Bitterly hating each other, and jealous of each other, they made war with their private armies and played at politics. Some of them declared they were loyal to the French King, Charles; but it was only for what they could get out of it. Others were even ready to form alliances with the English, if it would serve their own ambitions. The mighty Duke of Burgundy, who owned vast lands in eastern France, was entirely on the side of the English, and he had many supporters.

So with two kings who were not kings, and many nobles who tried to be kings, France was a sad place. Armies drifted from town to town, bands of men from village to village, and no-one really knew who ruled the land.

But Joan knew, because her Voices had told her. France belonged to the people of France, ruled over by the king made sacred by God. God did not want the English to remain on French soil; they should go back to England, the land God had given them. And if they would not go, it was right for the people of France to take up arms against them.

This was something quite new. The idea that the common people, villagers or townspeople, felt any patriotism, or had any say in who ruled them, or to whom the land belonged, was unheard of. They were thought no more important than the rabbits in a field, who feel nothing when the field is sold and they have a new 'owner'. France for the people of France was the new idea that Joan gave to France—and a great many people, like the English, and the French nobles and the princes of the church, who thought the people should obey them, did not like the new idea at all.

Joan listened to her Voices every day for five years, and learned from them that the English must be brushed aside and the Dauphin escorted to Reims to be crowned King. Then he would lead the armies of France, take possession of Paris, his capital city, and drive the English out of his kingdom.

For those five years, Joan stayed quietly, the good daughter sewing at home, waiting for the moment when her Voices should tell her that the time had come... the time for her to put on armour and ride to war, to save France and its King.

5. The mission

THOSE five years were a confused and disturbing time for Joan. She loved her Voices and was happy when they spoke to her, but she was still deeply puzzled when they insisted that the day would come when she must leave Domremy and lead the armies of France.

One day her father told them he had had a terrible dream. He pointed at Joan. 'I saw YOU,' he stormed, 'going off with a band of soldiers—leaving your respectable family to go to their camp like a loose woman. If that ever happens,' he threatened, 'I shall tell your brothers to take you away and drown you. And if they won't do it, I'll do it myself!'

In tears, Joan tried to tell him it was only a dream. But she knew all the time she was planning to go off with the soldiers, even if it was not quite as her father imagined.

France was still torn by the English armies of occupation; and now the fighting came very near Domremy, so that Joan's family and the other villagers took their cattle and goods and escaped to a nearby town. They lodged at an inn, and while they were there Joan helped the innkeeper, Madame La Rousse, with the work of the house. It was two weeks before it was safe for them to go home, and they found the church and many of the houses had been burnt and left in ruins.

Ever since his dream, Jacques d'Arc had wanted to see his daughter respectably married. Now, without asking her, he betrothed her to a local man. Since she had first heard her Voices, Joan had vowed she would not marry until God told her, through her Voices, that her mission was complete. She refused to have anything to do with the young man. He tried to bring a lawsuit against her, but she managed to escape from the arrangement.

News came that the English were now besieging the great city of Orleans, not far from Chinon, where the Dauphin held his court. The Voices told Joan it would be her task to end the siege of Orleans, and the time was drawing near.

Now, with the armies getting closer, and her parents urging her to marry, while at the same time her Voices encouraged her forward, Joan was under terrible pressure when she came to her seventeenth birthday in January of 1429. The Voices told her she must begin by going to the Governor in Vaucouleurs, and he would send her to the Dauphin.

This was the moment to set out. She told her mother she would go and stay with her cousin, Jeanne Laxart, who was going to have a baby, and help her in the house. Jeanne's husband, Durand, was fifteen years older then Joan, and she had always respectfully called him Uncle. He had always been very kind to her, and she was sure he would help her now. She did not tell her parents, or her brothers or Hauviette and her other friends, about her secret plans, but on a cold January day, wearing her shabby red dress, her dark hair long over her shoulders, Joan of Arc left Domremy for ever. The first stage in her journey took her only ten miles away, but it was the first important step on a journey that would take her miles across France.

She soon managed to persuade Durand to help her on her incredible quest. 'Joan told me she wanted to go into France to the Dauphin, to have him crowned,' he said simply, years later.

The first step was to go to Vaucouleurs, to speak to the Governor in his castle. He was Robert de Baudricourt, the man Joan's father had sometimes been to see on village business; and perhaps for this reason, he agreed to see her. She spoke steadfastly.

'I am come in the name of My Lord. The Kingdom of France belongs to him, but he wishes the Dauphin to rule as King. I am to make him King and lead him to his coronation.'

'Who is your Lord?' asked the amazed Lord Robert.

'The King of Heaven,' Joan replied simply.

The Governor thought she was mad—or making fun of him. Flabbergasted and angry, he roared to Durand to take her home to her father and tell him to give her a beating.

They slipped away to their lodging; but the townspeople got to know what Joan wanted, and began to support her. Lord Robert heard of this, and although he kept refusing Joan's pleas to see him again, he did write a letter to the Dauphin telling him about it, and asking if he wanted to see this extraordinary young woman.

When she still failed to see the Governor, Joan

decided she would wait for him no longer, but would set out alone, with Durand and a friend of his. She changed her old red dress for a shabby outfit of man's clothes. Travelling was dangerous for anyone in those troubled times, particularly for a young woman, and Joan sensibly thought she would be more secure dressed as a man. Uncle Durand got her a horse, and they set off.

By the first night they had got as far as a tiny wayside chapel, and Joan went inside to pray. There was a large and beautiful carved wooden crucifix, and Joan knelt for a long time, looking up at the crucified Christ. She remembered her Voices had told her she must wait at Vaucouleurs until she was given help to go forward. She felt it was wrong to go against her Voices at the very start of her mission, so they turned round and went back.

On February 12th, far away in Orleans in the west, there was a battle, and once more the French troops were defeated. The Voices told Joan about this, and she strode into the castle, and right into the presence of the Governor.

'You are delaying too long,' she said. 'Battles are being lost. You must send me to the Dauphin!'

He was half convinced, and at the same time, a messenger came from the Daphin with the reply to his own letter. 'Send the girl,' it said, 'unless you think she is working with evil spirits.'

That night as Joan sat in her lodging, de Baudricourt arrived, bringing a priest with him. 'If you are an evil spirit, leave me, said the priest. 'But if you are not, draw near!' Joan knelt down, and on her knees moved towards him. Joan's supporters and followers now believed firmly, like Joan herself, that the Voices were good spirits, sent from God;

but her enemies, especially the English, believed she was a witch, dealing with evil spirits and using black magic to help her against her enemies.

The priest reported that he did not believe Joan was a witch, and hastily Robert de Baudricourt promised to help her get to the royal court.

The people of Vaucouleurs were eager and excited. They gave Joan a new good suit of men's clothes, a black doublet and hose, a black cap and cape, and a grey top coat, and high brown boots. Men's clothes or not, they were the finest clothes Joan had ever worn in her life. And when she had asked a woman to cut her hair short, round her ears, she looked like a page boy in a lord's household.

Yet this too was to lead to trouble later. In those days all women wore long hair, and long skirts, too. To try to change, to dress like a man, was going against God's purpose for women. To look like a man—to stride out and face the world like a man— was considered to be a really wrong thing to do. All that trouble lay in the future; Joan was doing as her Voices ordered, and indeed she was only being sensible, for she could cross France more safely dressed as a man. It would be easier, even with her own bodyguard if she could get them right from the start to accept her as a fellow soldier and a comrade, not as a tiresome young woman.

The people of Vaucouleurs saw, like Joan, that it was a sensible step. They gave her a dagger; de Baudricourt gave her a horse and a sword, and an escort of six men, who swore they would take good care of Joan on the journey. He put letters for the Dauphin in Joan's hands.

They decided it would be safer to travel by night; and so in the early evening twilight, on February 23rd, 1429, they gathered in the courtyard of the Governor's castle. Durand and many of the townspeople clustered round to say Goodbye and Godspeed.

'Aren't you affaid the enemy will attack you?' they asked her.

'I am not afraid of them,' she said, 'I have a safe road, for I have God with me, who will prepare my way to the Dauphin. To do this was I born!'

The little company of seven riders set out from the courtyard into the gathering darkness.

6. The Dauphin at Chinon

JOAN and her escort took eleven days to cross war-torn France from Vaucouleurs to Chinon, travelling by night, sleeping up by day, always at risk from attacks on the way. During that time the Dauphin waited for her, without any particular impatience, at his castle of Chinon, which was about 150 miles from Paris, the capital city which would not accept him.

Nine years older than Joan, he was twenty-six years old now. With a thick nose and heavy lips, and a shambling walk, he had been called the ugliest man in France.

He was unfortunate in other ways, too. His mother had agreed to a treaty with the English, and to support it she had declared that her son Charles had no right to rule. He was nervous and unwarlike, and dared not venture as far as Reims to be crowned. He was so doubtful of himself that even his supporters and advisers spoke to him scornfully.

His vagueness and fearfulness, his unwillingness ever to make up his mind, were a total contrast to Joan, with her sturdy common sense and shining certainty that God and her Voices would bring everything to a good end.

Even when Joan arrived at Chinon, she was kept waiting for two days before the Dauphin would see her—and still he hesitated. Then he told one of his courtiers to take his place on the throne while he hid behind a pillar.

'If God is guiding her,' he said, half joking, 'let us see if he guides her to me.'

Joan strode in to the great hall and looked about her. The court ladies in their high headdresses and long skirts giggled at her short hair and travel-stained page's suit. The men stared curiously at the young girl who promised to win their battles for them. Joan gave one look at the man seated on the throne, then plunged into the crowd.

'God give you health, noble Dauphin,' she said as she knelt before him. She knew him directly, and the joke, if it was a joke, had fallen flat. She told him she had come with a message from God—she was to end the siege of Orleans and see the Dauphin crowned.

He took her aside, ready to believe her now, and led her into the chapel. She talked to him and made him see that she truly believed he was the king God meant to rule France.

The Dauphin led Joan back to the court, and she stood at his side while he told everyone he had accepted her as his adviser. She thought this meant that everyone would be ready to rush forward at once, to set out for Orleans the next day. She still knew nothing about court officials and the delays they could set up.

She told them that she was the Maid—the pure young girl chosen by God to carry out his will. She

was treated very kindly, given rooms in the castle, with a page boy to wait on her, and her own tiny chapel, and a chaplain to say Mass for her and hear her confessions. She was allowed to see the Dauphin when she wished, and she got to know his followers. Some of them became her friends. His cousin, the Duke of Alencon, she always called My fine Duke; and he gave her a horse as a present. But while most of the court thought she was amusing, and rather touching, they had no intention of taking her seriously.

The Dauphin's advisers, and perhaps the Dauphin himself, were still full of doubts. It was after all a big thing to give this unknown village girl a say in fighting battles, and they kept setting up tests for her.

A group of respectable women was ordered to carry out a medical examination, to see if she was really the young girl she claimed to be. Then one day she was told she was being taken on an expedition; she believed it was Orleans at last, but on the road she was told they were going to Poictiers.

'I know there is trouble waiting for me there,' she said, 'but my Voices will help me, so let us go.'

In Poictiers she found a council of clergy and learned doctors of the church gathered to question her about her Voices—more and more about her Voices. Their aim was to see if Joan was making up her stories, or if she was a witch dealing with bad spirits who would destroy them all. It was the first time she had ever spoken out in public about her Voices, and she tried to stay calm, though sometimes she spoke impatiently.

They asked her what language the Voices spoke in. Of course it was French; she did not know any other. What sort of French? 'Better than yours,' she flashed. There was laughter in court, as that judge spoke with a thick local accent.

They asked her for some proof, that her Voices came from God. 'I have not come here to perform signs,' she retorted 'Let me get to Orleans, and I will show you why I am sent.'

'Surely, if God really wishes to free the people of France, he does not need armies?'

'The soldiers will fight,' declared Joan staunchly, 'and God will give them victory.'

Every question and answer was written down and put on record. But soon afterwards the record vanished, and no trace of it has ever been seen. Yet it was an important state document, and its disappearance is one of the strangest of the mysteries about Joan of Arc.

At last they believed her. Orleans, after all, was in real danger, and the Dauphin had very few other supporters. The judges stated that they did not believe she was a witch, and that it would be in order for the Dauphin to allow her to help him.

Now that the church doctors said they believed in her, everyone believed in her. She was given a suit of shining silver armour, a black war horse and a banner that she chose herself, with a picture of Christ holding the world in his hands, and two angels, one of them giving him a fleur de lys, the emblem of France.

She said she needed a sword, and told them they would find one hidden behind the altar in the church of St Catherine at Furbois. No one had ever heard of it, but they did everything she asked now, so they looked—and there it was. She was equipped and ready to set out for Orleans, at the head of the army of France. She was joyful and hopeful, believing with all her heart that with the help of God and her Voices she was leading the army to victory.

7. *The Maid of Orleans*

ORLEANS was a large and important town on a bend of the River Loire, which runs from east to west across France. It was loyal to the Dauphin, but for eight months, since the last October, English armies had lain outside its walls. It was possible for people to slip in and out of the town, even to get some food in. But the English armies were there to prevent French troops getting in, and would certainly seize any large supplies of food meant for the townspeople. This was a problem, as people from the surrounding countryside had flocked into Orleans for safety and the city was crammed with fifty thousand people.

So the Dauphin was cut off from one of his most important towns, and the English armies barred the road to Reims, where he must go to be crowned. Orleans was vital to the French and to the English armies. If the English could seize it, they could thrust their armies forward and soon the whole of France would be in their hands; and if Charles the

Dauphin lost it, he would have no defence left against the English, and would have lost everything. That was why Joan's Voices told her that if she was to save France, as God willed, she must begin by saving Orleans.

Joan and her army arrived outside Orleans towards the end of April. They brought supplies of food for the trapped townspeople, and took up position on the banks of the Loire, a few miles upstream from Orleans. The plan was to bring barges up from Orleans, load them with food, then send them back down river to the city. Yet for days an easterly wind had blown towards the city, so the barges could not move against the wind, upstream to where the supplies were waiting.

Joan stood on the bank, asking why there was a delay. She was told the wind was against them.

'Don't worry about that!' she said. 'The wind will

soon change!'

Even as she spoke, the fluttering flags and banners, tossed by the wind, drooped and were still. Then they fluttered again; but this time they were blown by a westerly wind. Soon the barges reached them, and quickly the French troops loaded them with the precious food. Now the current could take them back downstream, and soon they reached the walls of Orleans safely.

The people of Orleans were as pleased to see the food as the soldiers, and they believed the Maid had worked a miracle for them.

Joan planned to get into the city itself with some of her troops, leaving the rest to attack the English outside. She crossed the river by boat with a force of two hundred men. The next evening, in the growing darkness, she entered Orleans. She wore her shining armour and rode a white horse, and her

banner was carried before her. The people of Orleans really believed that God had sent her to save them. She was received as a deliverer, as if the city had already been rescued from the English. People poured out to welcome her, though it was raining hard. The rain cleared, and they lit torches and led her in procession through the streets. Men, women and children poured out of their houses and crowded forward, trying to touch her, or her horse. One of the torches set fire to the banner, but Joan turned her horse and quickly put it out herself.

All the time she was with the army, Joan was concerned with the soldiers. If they were to carry out God's work, they must be good men. She insisted they should give up foul language and drunken and violent behaviour, and should go to confession and attend Mass regularly.

She had no wish to kill even the English soldiers, if it could be avoided; so she opened her attack by writing a letter to the English Commander—or rather, had someone else write one for her, as she never learned to read or write. 'I don't know A from B,' she said. 'Write this for me: "Duke of Bedford, calling yourself Regent of France. Deliver up the keys of all the good towns in France you have taken, to the Maid, who has been sent by God, the king of Heaven. For God's sake, go back to England!"'

Not surprisingly, the English commanders ignored all her letters. The English had been ready to play a waiting game outside Orleans, for time was on their side, but now Joan was in the city they launched a fierce attack to destroy her and capture the city once and for all. For her part, Joan wanted to strike quickly. Soon ladders and platforms were pushed against the city walls from the inside, and men mounted them, shooting arrows on the English outside, while the English were firing down and trying to get into the town. There were days of fighting, the English thrusting forward to get into the city, the French struggling desperately to keep them out, and to drive them out of their strongholds.

Joan was everywhere, wherever the fighting was fiercest. She inspired the French troops and the people of Orleans, so that time and time again the enemy attack was beaten off.

Yet even now the French commanders could not trust her completely. They held a war council without Joan, deciding to wait for reinforcements before they attacked again.

Joan was furious. This was not the council her Voices had given her.

'The Council of God will triumph,' she declared. 'We will fight tomorrow. I shall have great things to do—but blood will flow from my body, above the breast.'

Her enthusiasm forced them forward, and next day fighting was fiercer than ever. But another prophecy came true, because she was wounded by an arrow which struck her above the breast and made a wound six inches deep. At first she was frightened and upset, but as soon as the wound had been dressed, she bravely went back to the action.

Then once more she could be seen in the heart of the action in her shining silver armour, with her banner always held close behind her. The French troops felt they could not be beaten so long as she was there leading them, while the English troops were beginning to feel they could not win while Joan the Maid led the forces of France. They looked for a way to withdraw, and when the French towed a barge full of kindling under the wooden drawbridge, and set fire to it, they feared they would be cut off completely. They hurried to get out of Orleans, back to their camp. They did not stay there, but were soon on their way, leaving the freed city of Orleans behind them. For the first time for eight months there were no English troops outside its walls.

The bells in the churches rang, and soldiers and townspeople gave thanks to God and to the Maid he had sent to them.

Joan had done the first thing her Voices had commanded: she had ended the siege of Orleans, and she had inflicted a great defeat on the English. And she had made herself a name in history... from now on she was the Maid of Orleans.

8. The coronation

NOW THAT the siege of Orleans was over and the English armies had gone, the way lay open between Chinon, where the Dauphin was, and the city of Reims, with its cathedral. Nothing lay between the Dauphin and his coronation—nothing except the Dauphin himself. He thanked Joan, and congratulated her, but he made no haste to move. Joan was passionately eager to follow up the military success of the relief of Orleans, by carrying on attacks against the English, so that they would be forced to leave France altogether, and she was desperate to have the coronation take place.

She knelt in front of the Dauphin and pleaded with him: 'Noble Dauphin, come to Reims at once to receive the crown. My Voices urge me to this most of all.'

She believed that once the Dauphin was crowned, he would become a holy person, consecrated to God, so that his enemies would lose their power. His advisers agreed with her, but they wanted more towns along the river Loire safe in French hands before they ventured to Reims.

So Joan led the army again, in a series of successful battles. She was so successful during these long summer days that they were called her Week of Victories. She forced the English to withdraw, and captured towns they had held, so that town after town was back under the Dauphin's rule. None of them was so important as Orleans, but their capture showed the Battle of Orleans was not just a single success, but that the Maid could really win battles.

More and more the French troops and the French people believed that Joan was sent from God to save them, while the English became angrier and angrier at her triumphs, and said she won her battles through black magic and evil spirits.

It was not until July 17th—three months after she had saved Orleans—that her dream came true. Then at last, with majestic and impressive ceremony, the timid Dauphin was crowned King of France, like all his ancestors before him. When he was anointed with the holy oil, given, it was said, by St Remy himself, he knew, and Joan knew, and all the people of France knew, that he was the true King of France—King Charles VII.

Joan was there to see the second command of her Voices fulfilled. She had ended the siege of Orleans, and now the Dauphin was crowned King. Throughout the ceremony she stood beside the Dauphin, wearing her shining armour and holding aloft her banner with the figure of Christ between the angels and the lilies of France. 'It stood up to the battle—it deserves the honour now,' she said. She knelt before the newly crowned monarch and called him King. He was her Dauphin no longer.

It was her finest moment as she stood, the Maid of Orleans, who had been the instrument of God's purpose, and she thanked God for her Voices who had made His amazing plan clear to her.

Her father, Jacques d'Arc, made the journey from Domremy to Reims and met his daughter again. It was hardly six months since she had left home, but for both of them it must have seemed a lifetime ago. When he saw her in her shining armour, next to the King, or talking to the leaders of the army, did he remember his threat that he would drown her if she went away with the soldiers? The king made him a present of money, and agreed to a request from Joan that the village of Domremy should no longer be taxed—a promise the kings of France kept for three hundred and fifty years.

Even among the festivity, Joan could not forget there was more to do. The King could not enter Paris, his capital, for France was in the hands of the English and the Burgundians, the armies of the Duke of Burgundy who supported the English against the King of France. Once more impatient to follow up a success, Joan urged the King and the army leaders to march on Paris forthwith.

9. On to Paris

AT LAST, once again slowly and grudgingly, the King gave Joan permission to fight his battles for him. Yet even as she set out, his advisers, who stayed behind—no friends to Joan and her driving energy—urged him to another, less courageous plan. He signed an agreement with the Duke of Burgundy.

Unknowing, Joan reached the walls of Paris and the great Abbey of St Denis, which housed sacred relics of St Denis, patron saint of France, and where all the kings of France came at last to be buried. To Joan it was a place almost as wonderful as the cathedral at Reims, and she dreamed of entering Paris through the great gate of St Denis, leading the King in triumph.

He had promised to join her there, and he arrived, eventually, on September 7th. Joan had already carried out preliminary attacks to test the English defences, and she was sure they would succeed. She spent that night in prayer, expecting a decisive battle the next day. In the morning she went forth at the head of her army, to recapture Paris.

It was a difficult assault, for they did not know the ground, and the troops were lost among the narrow twisting streets. They did not feel they were making progress, although the English and the Burgundians were slowly retreating before them.

Suddenly Joan was struck down, wounded by an arrow which pierced her thigh, and her standard bearer, who carried her banner into battle, was killed. She was carried off the battlefield, protesting all the time that she could carry on, that soon the city would be theirs and they would achieve a victory. As she was carried away, the heart seemed to go out of the French attack, and soon the generals called off the troops, saying they would make a fresh start the next day.

In the morning Joan was ready to lead them forward when a message came from the King himself. He ordered the army to withdraw, and commanded Joan and the other generals to join him at St Denis. If they were ordered to withdraw by the King, they had no choice; but they had one hope left. They had hastily built a bridge over the River Seine, and they believed they could yet use it to carry on the onslaught into the city. But they found it had been destroyed in the night by the orders of the King. It seems clear that the King had promised the Duke of Burgundy not to carry through with the attack on Paris, and the Duke promised not to attack the French troops.

Joan, who knew nothing of this, was heartbroken, and utterly despondent. 'In God's name, the city might have been taken,' she cried. But it was not to be. She crept into the Abbey of St Denis and laid her shining armour before the statue of Our

Lady. She felt she would never need it again; and perhaps too she felt that now she would never be able to carry out the last two commands of her Voices, to capture Paris and drive the English out of France.

It did not all end at St Denis. Fighting went on; Joan had not fought her last battle, and wherever she appeared the people of France received her as an honoured guest. Yet the joyful certainty of the early days had gone. She knew she could be wounded, and she knew that in spite of her Voices she could be forced to give up before she won a victory.

The next May, she was expecting the English to attack the important town of Compiegne, so she took her army to help the townspeople. The end came outside the gates of Compiegne. She led a small troop outside the town gates to attack the English as they arrived.

As Joan and a handful of soldiers waited, suddenly the great gates banged shut so that they could no longer get back into the town. No one has ever been sure if this was an act of treachery by the governor of Compiegne, or if he thought the enemy troops were going to storm the open gate and burst into the town, and that is why he ordered the gates to be closed. But Joan and her handful were cut off, beyond help, and at the mercy of the enemy.

Amazed at their good luck, a troop of Burgundians rushed forward and surrounded Joan. An archer seized her and dragged her from her horse. Her troops could not help her, and there was no attempt to rescue her from Compiegne—the town gates stayed shut. She was helpless, a captive in the

hands of the Burgundians, allies of the English who had sworn to have her put to death.
    It was just a year since she had freed Orleans.

10. Capture

THE SOLDIER who had captured her handed her over to his officer, who gave her to his overlord. Soon she was in the hands of Jean of Luxembourg, a supporter of the Duke of Burgundy. For the next few months she was moved from one lord to another, from castle to castle, while they decided what to do with her.

If the King had offered money for her now, he could have bought her back and set her free. Even later, the French could have made a treaty with the Duke of Burgundy, or the English leader, the Duke of Bedford, if they had solemnly promised that Joan would not go to war against them again. Or the King could have ordered his generals, men who had fought alongside Joan in his battles, to gather their troops and mount an all-out attack to rescue her. It might not have worked, but it would have been better than leaving her a helpless prisoner.

He never did. In all the dreadful year after she was first captured, the King made no attempt to ransom her or rescue her, and seemed hardly concerned about what was happening to her.

At first she was kindly treated, visited by the Burgundian generals and their wives. The ladies urged Joan to grow her hair and put on women's clothes again, and they offered her dresses of their own. But she still refused, saying her Voices told her not to. Certainly now that she was guarded by enemy soldiers it was sensible not to appear as a woman.

Despairing of being saved by her friends, Joan tried to escape; although she said her Voices had not told her to. She once tried to escape from a fifty-foot tower: she fell and was knocked unconscious, but she was not otherwise hurt.

These months revealed her enemies. One of the most bitter was Robert Cauchon, the Bishop of Beauvais. He was totally on the side of the English, and he bargained with the Burgundians, so that for money they handed Joan over to the English. Cauchon was determined to accuse Joan of being a witch and put her on trial, with himself as her judge. He arranged that she should be taken to Normandy, which was entirely in English hands. As reward for all this, he hoped to be made Archbishop of Rouen.

In December of 1431, Joan and her captors finally got to Rouen. It was nearly two years since she had left Domremy, and during that time she had travelled three thousand miles through France. Now she was within a few hundred yards of the place where she would die.

11. The prisoner on trial

IT WAS Christmas time, and the most wretched months of her life lay ahead. Until she was seventeen, Joan had been free, at home, in her father's garden, in the fields around Domremy—free to go to the village church, and free to listen to her Voices.

Then for eighteen months she had lived in a blaze of glory; she was the Maid of Orleans, riding out boldly to war, living as no other woman had lived.

The last months, since she had been a captive, had been bad—deserted and betrayed by friends, uncertain of the future, moved from prison to prison—but at least she had moved around, and had felt the sun and wind on her face. And her Voices had spoken to her.

Now everything was changed. Kept in a narrow cell, sometimes chained in her place, watched day and night by coarse and mocking English soldiers who were her guards, her condition was miserable indeed. But that was not the worst. She was the prisoner of the Church; and the Church declared she was unworthy of all the comforts of her faith. She might not receive Holy Communion, nor hear

Mass, nor go to confession. In the depths of her despair, her Voices did not come to comfort her.

That was how she lived. But she was not only a prisoner—she was a prisoner on trial for her life. Each day she was taken from her cell to face a courtroom of accusers eager to find her guilty of crimes for which she could be sent to a horrible death. The English were determined she would be condemned as a witch, for that would excuse their own defeats and would end all the French support and belief in her.

The Bishop of Beauvais, her great enemy, was

the chief of her judges, and there were men representing the authorities of the Church. But as the trial took place in English-held Rouen, with the English lords demanding a death sentence on Joan after she had been discredited as a witch, it was impossible for her to receive a fair trial. In a way her judges, like Joan herself, were prisoners of the English soldiers who guarded the courtroom and the town of Rouen.

Utterly alone, Joan tried to stay calm and brave, and to answer all the questions truthfully. One thing was clear to her—she must never deny her Voices, or say that they were not sent to her directly from God.

She was asked about every detail of her life, back to her years as a child. Even the story of dancing round the fairy tree was raked up and held against her: they said it showed that even as a child she had had dealings with evil spirits.

For hour after hour she was asked about her Voices. When had she first heard them? What did they look like? What did they tell her? Why did she say they came from God? Joan replied that they had always spoken to her about God, and had never told her to do anything against his word. They told her God had a special mission for her.

The judges seized on that. Surely this mission was against God's will? Because of course the English could not admit for a moment that it was God's will that they should be driven out of France!

Joan reminded them that she had answered all these questions before, at the inquiry at Poictiers, when the judges had decided that her Voices really came from God. All the proceedings then had been written down; she begged her present judges to read it. But the report had conveniently been lost, and her judges refused to consider it.

They went back to her mission. She had dressed as a man, and cut her hair short. That was surely wicked and indecent, and against everything God wanted women to do. Her Voices had told her to behave like that, she protested; and if she was to go among men and to lead soldiers, it made good sense. A woman should not go among men and lead soldiers, thundered the judges; and they declared she would not be allowed to hear Mass again until she dressed as a woman. She replied that if they guaranteed she could hear Mass, she would put on a

woman's dress; but they would make her no promises.

People believed that no witch could manage to say the Our Father without stumbling over the words, and the court kept trying to make Joan say the prayer. She refused to say it before them all, but begged that a priest should hear her confession, and said she would say the Our Father to him. They refused her this comfort too.

Once the court spoke of the King, and said that since his dealings with Joan he too should be declared a heretic and cut off by the Church. Joan defended him. 'Speak of me, not of the King! I dare

swear that my King is the most noble Christian of all Christians!' she flashed—about the King who had sent no word to her all the dreadful year she had been in prison. Joan sometimes spoke so well that even her judges were impressed. Once they asked her if, accused of so many crimes, she could possibly believe that she was in a state of grace. 'If I am, may God keep me there, and if not, may he put me there!' she said.

Taken from her cell each day to face hours of remorseless questioning by her hostile judges, then back to her prison at night, to the coarse treatment of the English soldiers, not allowed to go to Mass or confession, threatened with a horrible death and with torture; at last she broke down.

Yes, she agreed, if the Bishops and clergy told her she was wicked, they must be right. Yes, if they said her Voices had not come from God, she would agree with them. Yes, she would put on woman's clothes. Yes, she would sign a statement saying she would submit to the court and set aside her evil ways.

Warwick and the English lords were angry, thinking she had slipped through their fingers; but Cauchon told them to be patient for a little while.

Next day, Joan dutifully looked for the woman's dress to put on, as she had promised; but it was not there. All she had to wear was her man's dress again, knowing that her judges would declare she had disobeyed them.

Back in court, she was asked if she had heard her Voices again, since she had submitted to the judges. Yes, she answered, they had spoken to her. She had only turned away from them because she was frightened. They had told her she had not done well, but that they brought her the mercy of God.

This was a fatal answer, and the judges were delighted. By once more owning her Voices, and claiming they came from God, Joan had wiped out everything she had said when she gave in to the Court. Now they could claim that she had for a moment repented of her sin, but had relapsed into it again. They need make no pretence of showing mercy now.

Eagerly Cauchon set his hand to the parchment declaring that the woman Joan was to appear before him the next morning in the market place at Rouen, where she would be declared cut off from the Church and handed over to the officers of the law, to be put to death by burning.

12. The end

WHEN Joan heard how she was to die, she was very frightened. 'I would rather be beheaded seven times, than burnt,' she cried pitifully. She spent the last night in prison, as quietly as she could, trying to be brave, trying to pray. In the morning, two priests came and heard her confession. In a merciful moment, Cauchon had agreed that she might receive Holy Communion, which she

had been refused all those months in prison. It was brought to her, but hastily, without respect. One of the priests protested, and candles were brought, and a stole for the priest, and so she received the Blessed Sacrament.

'Where shall I be tonight?' she asked suddenly. 'Have you no faith in Our Lord?' asked the priest gently. 'Yes,' she said. 'God helping me, I shall be with him in Paradise.'

Cauchon came to see her in prison. 'Bishop, I die through you,' she declared; and she told him he should have kept her in a church prison, with proper keepers, not in a cell guarded by common soldiers.

She was calm and steady now, and put on a long robe that was brought to her, and a hood. Then she was taken in a cart for her last journey. At nine in the morning of May 30th, as the bells in the churches rang, she was led into the market square, accompanied by the priests, and with a guard of soldiers, to face the watching crowds, and the waiting flames.

13. Joan of France

IN THE years that followed, many people believed Joan had been treated cruelly and unjustly. Eighteen years later, the French recaptured the city of Rouen from the English and King Charles ordered that an inquiry should be held into every detail of her trial. Cauchon by that time was dead; but it was found that he and the other judges had made up their minds to find Joan guilty and put her to death. She had not had a fair trial.

Twenty-five years after she was burnt at Rouen by orders of the Church, the church authorities declared that the judgement had been wrong; Joan was not guilty of all the crimes she had been accused of, and she should never have been put to death. In one way, of course, it was too late; but it meant a great deal to Joan's family and supporters, and it was an encouragement to the French forces.

Joan's Dauphin, whom she saw crowned as King Charles VII, ruled for thirty years after her death, and his descendants were kings of France for more than three hundred years.

Soon after Joan's death, England was torn by a

civil war that nearly destroyed the country. One by one all the English possessions in France were lost, and by the end of the next century England owned no more land in France.

In the long years since then, the English have changed their minds about Joan of Arc. Now they believe that she was truthful and brave, and that her Voices spoke to her from God. They are sorry the English put her on trial and sent her to her death, and they like to remember the English soldier who gave her a cross at the very end.

The ordinary people of France had always known that Joan, the Maid of France, was sent to them by God. After her death, they asked her to pray for them, believing that her prayers would protect France and keep their own loved ones safe in battle. They were told that now it was suitable that statues of her, and memorial crosses, should be put up to her, and a great many appeared—including a great statue of her on a horse where she fought her greatest battle, in Orleans. Today her statue stands in churches and cathedrals all over France. They show a young girl, dressed in armour like a knight, sometimes holding up a sword like a cross, or a banner. Often the artist has given her a kind of skirt over the armour, which looks strange; for certainly Joan never wore one. Still, it makes it easy to tell who the statue is supposed to be!

Nearly five hundred years after her death in the market place at Rouen, during which the people had honoured her with their prayers, the church finally honoured Joan with its greatest recognition and she was declared a saint, with a special day for her to be remembered, on the anniversary of her death. Then she was declared the Patron Saint of France, along with Saint Denis.

Joan did not believe she was an ordinary woman; she believed that God, for reasons of His own, had chosen her for a special purpose, and had spoken to her by His messengers. She believed that God meant each country to be ruled and governed by its own people, not by invading foreigners. She showed that God did not always want women to stay sheltered at home or in convents, but to go out to meet the world and its problems. And she believed, right up to her death, that someone might have a direct command from God, and that command must be obeyed, however much church and governments, kings and bishops, tried to prevent it.

That is why Joan, the peasant girl who lived and died more than five hundred and fifty years ago, is still honoured. It is why she is a saint for today.